HOT CARS

MERCEDES-AMG GT

Judy Greenspan

rourkeeducationalmedia.com

TABLE OF CONTENTS

NOT YOUR FAMILY MINIVAN

Imagine a hot summer day. You're old enough to drive and heading to the beach. Do you want to bring your friends? Sports gear? Plenty of food? Then take the family minivan and leave the Mercedes-AMG GT at home.

Or, pick one friend and go in style! The AMG GT is a super-fast sports car with room inside for only two. Some call this powerful car "aggressive," "breathtaking," and "a piece of art." Others simply say, "wow!"

Built for speed, the AMG GT is shaped like a race car and drives like one too. Long, wide, and not very tall, it tears around the racetrack at nearly 190 miles (306 kilometers) per hour. How fast is that? Faster than a Category 5 hurricane wind!

DM·907·FR

With a racing car's lightweight **chassis**, large tires, and low center of gravity, the AMG GT is designed to take tight turns at top speeds and keep its balance.

But the AMG GT is not only for racing. It's also made for everyday driving. That's right, you can take this speedster on the road, so prepare for adventure.

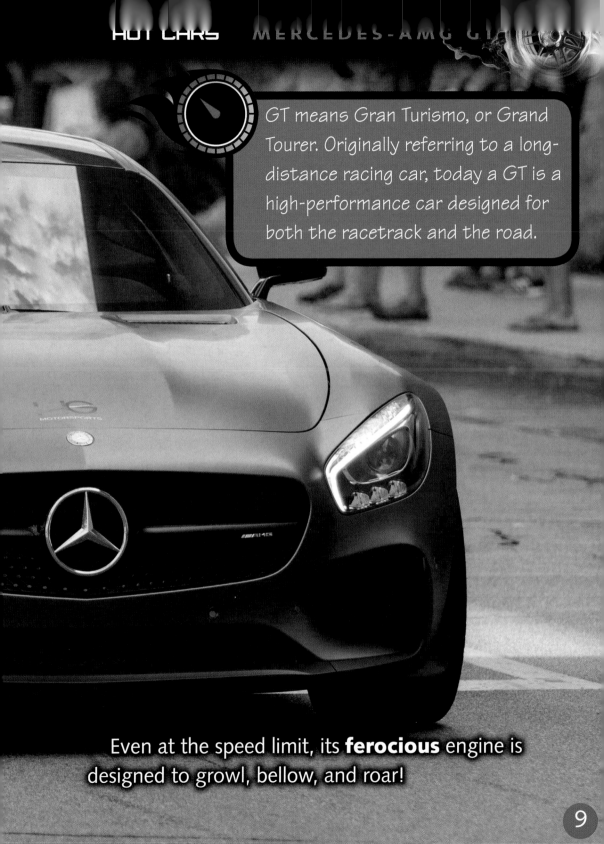

GT means Gran Turismo, or Grand Tourer. Originally referring to a long-distance racing car, today a GT is a high-performance car designed for both the racetrack and the road.

Even at the speed limit, its **ferocious** engine is designed to growl, bellow, and roar!

Can you say "four-liter biturbo V8 engine" out loud? Sounds powerful and it is! The AMG GT engine produces a fierce 456 **horsepower** and 443 pound-feet (600.6 Newton-meters) of torque. Horsepower and torque are **measurements** of an engine's strength. The bigger the numbers, the stronger the engine. So fire it up and fasten your seatbelt! This car speeds up, or accelerates, from zero to 60 miles (96.6 kilometers) per hour in less than four seconds.

Why "Horsepower?"
In the late 1700s, the inventor James Watt created a new unit of measurement. He called it horsepower. Why? He was comparing the power of his new steam engine to something familiar: the number of horses, or horsepower, needed to do the same amount of work.

ONE EXPERT, ONE ENGINE

Every AMG engine also has a personal touch. Do you see the signature on the engine cover? At the AMG factory in Affalterbach, Germany, one **technician assembles** the entire engine, from start to finish. When the work is done, he or she proudly signs the finished product.

Only technicians with years of experience work in the Mercedes-AMG engine shop.

Inside the car, the driver controls that mighty engine with the push of a button. You can fine-tune the engine's performance for different speeds and road conditions. You can even crank up the exhaust to a thundering roar—but please, don't wake the neighbors!

Not surprisingly, driving an AMG GT takes some practice. For that, drivers can attend the AMG Driving Academy. Imagine a camp for the car-crazy! The academy offers instruction from how to control the car, to the high-level training needed for a racing license.

From the driver's seat, you'll feel like you're in the cockpit of a race car. Look at all those control buttons on the center console!

SPEED DEMONS

The Mercedes-AMG GT continues a long tradition of Mercedes Benz sports cars. Today, AMG is part of Mercedes Benz, but the company also has a long history of its own.

Karl Benz (sometimes spelled Carl)
1844 – 1929

Karl Benz invented the world's first automobile in Germany. But in 1888, he still wasn't sure if his new car could drive long distances. So Bertha Benz, his wife, secretly tested the vehicle. The car worked. She drove more than 100 miles (161 kilometers). Her husband was convinced. And the rest, as they say, is history.

The Benz Patent-Motorwagen Number 3 of 1886, used by Bertha Benz for the highly publicized first long-distance road trip.

Bertha Benz
1849 – 1944

...me joke that AMG means "Absolute Machir...

...s" or "Advanced Mechanical Gurus." But no...

abbreviation for the company's founders,

...er Aufrecht and Erhard Melcher, and Großas...

...German town where Aufrecht was born.

...unded in 1967, AMG originally built race ca...

...es. In 1971, they put their engine in a Merc...

...and made headlines. Their creation, the Me...

...SEL 6.8, was famously known as the "Red Pi...

...n German, the "Red Pig" is called the *Rote Sau*.

...6   AMG rolled out what would become a leg...

...mer. Fueled by an AMG 385 horsepower eng...

...door Mercedes whipped around the racetrac...

1998 At a blistering pace of 198 miles (318.7 kilometers) per hour and a whopping cost of $1,547,620 Mercedes Benz CLK GTR broke records in speed and price. It was named the most expensive car in the world by the 1998 *Guinness World Book of Records.*

Mercedes Benz CLK GTR

1990s AMG and Mercedes became official partners.

2009 The SLS was the first Mercedes Benz-AMG built from scratch. Customers loved the car's gull-wing doors.

SLS, stands for Sport Light Super or in German, *Sport Leicht Super.*

The hinges of a gull-wing door are on the roof of the car, not on the side.

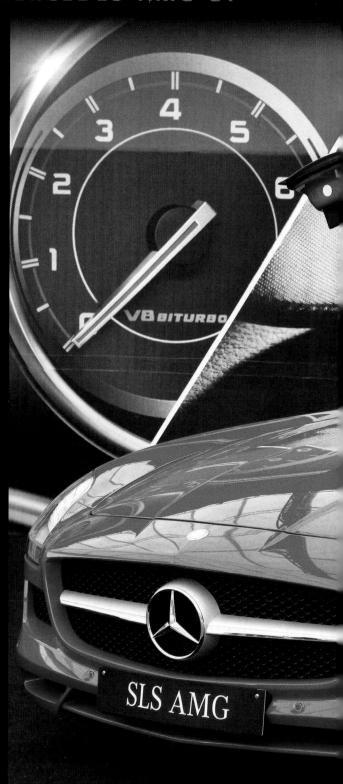

SLS AMG

2014 Advertised as "handcrafted by racers" the GT was the second car AMG completely designed.

AMG GT S

Just as there are different versions of the iPhone, there are variations on the AMG GT. They include the GT S, GT C, and GT R. Some are bigger, some are faster, and all of them cost more than $100,000.

Mercedes-AMG GT S

Sporting flashy twin 5-spoke wheels, the GTS is a hair faster than the GT, accelerating from zero to 60 miles (96.6 kilometers) per hour in 3.7 seconds compared to 3.9.

Mercedes-AMG GT S

Mercedes-AMG GT C

Hold onto your hats! A convertible with a 550-horsepower engine, the GTC is more powerful than the standard GT and 2.2 inches (5.6 centimeters) wider as well.

AMG GT C Roadster

Mercedes-AMG GT R

It weighs less than the GT S but the GT R is the most powerful member of the AMG GT family, clocking nearly 198 miles (318 kilometers) per hour on the racetrack.

DRIVING INTO THE FUTURE

To keep up with competitors like Audi R8, BMWi8, Jaguar F-TYPE, Porsche 911, and Corvette Z06, AMG makes sure their cars can handle every **terrain** and temperature.

As the AMG GT drives into the future, what can fans expect to see next? Some would like more leg room. Others want a softer seat. But one thing is for sure. Mercedes AMG is already working on an even faster car. So keep your seatbelt fastened!

Concept Cars

If you visit an auto show, chances are you'll see a concept car. Flashy and futuristic, these cars are so cool you might want to buy one. But concept cars are not for sale. They're only made to test new ideas. If enough customers give a thumbs up, the car could be made for real.

The Mercedes-AMG GT concept car, unveiled in 2017, is a four-door sports car with plenty of room inside for friends and luggage.

GLOSSARY

abbreviation (uh-bree-vee-AY-shun): a short way of writing a word or name

assembles (uh-SEM-buhlz): to put together the parts of something

chassis (CHASS-ee): the frame on which the body of a vehicle is built

ferocious (fuh-ROH-shuhss): very fierce

horsepower (HORSS-pou-ur): a unit for measuring the power of an engine

measurements (MEZH-ur-ments): the size, length, or amount of something, as established by measuring

technician (tek-NISH-uhn): someone who works with special equipment or does practical laboratory work

terrain (tuh-RAYN): ground or land

INDEX

SHOW WHAT YOU KNOW

1. Why do AMG technicians sign the engine?
2. What did Karl Benz invent?
3. What does AMG GT stand for?
4. What was the Red Pig?
5. Which car is listed in the 1998 *Guinness World Book of Records*?

WEBSITES TO VISIT

www.sciencekids.co.nz/videos/engineering/carengine.html

www://autoworld.com/mercedes/history/company/people-benz-bertha/people-benz-bertha.html

www://encyclopedia.kids.net.au/page/ho/Horsepower

ABOUT THE AUTHOR

Although Judy Greenspan likes adventure, she has never driven at 190 miles per hour and never will. However, she enjoyed learning about the Mercedes-AMG GT and how top-notch cars are designed. Judy is a former television producer and lives in New York City with her husband and two daughters.

Meet The Author!
www.meetREMauthors.com

www.rourkeeducationalmedia.com

PHOTO CREDITS: Cover © Global Communications Mercedes-Benz Cars; page 2-3 © EvrenKalinbacak - Shuttersyock; page 4-5 and 6-7 © Thesupermat https://creativecommons.org/licenses/by-sa/4.0/deed.en ; page 8-9 © betto rodrigues - Shutterstock, page 10-11 © Trybex - Shutterstock, page 12-13 © Teddy Leung - Shutterstock, page 14-15 © VanderWolf Images; page 18 © Grzegorz Czapski, 19 © Fingerhut - both from Shutterstock; page 20-21 Ovu0ng - Shutterstock; page 22-23 g Ed Aldridge - Shutterstock; Page 24-25 © Bahooka https://creativecommons.org/licenses/by-sa/4.0/deed.en ; Page 26-27 © Frederic Legrand - COMEO - Shutterstock; page 27 © Miro Vrlik Photography - Shutterstock; page 28-29 © lev radin - Shutterstock

Edited by: Keli Sipperley

Cover design by Rhea Magaro
Interior design by: Nicola Stratford   www.nicolastratford.com

Library of Congress PCN Data

Mercedes-AMG GT / Judy Greenspan
(VROOM! Hot Cars)
ISBN 978-1-68342-365-2 (hard cover)
ISBN 978-1-68342-531-1 (e-Book)
Library of Congress Control Number: 2017931202

Rourke Educational Media
Printed in the United States of America, North Mankato, Minnesota